Plan B

Julia A. Royston
BA, MA, MLS, DRE

ROYSTON
Publishing

BK Royston Publishing
P. O. Box 4321
Jeffersonville, IN 47131
502-802-5385
http://www.bkroystonpublishing.com
bkroystonpublishing@gmail.com

© Copyright – 2019

All Rights Reserved. No part of this book may be reproduced, stored in a retrieval system, or transmitted by any means without the written permission of the author.

Cover Design: Gad Savage, Elite Covers

ISBN-13: 978-1-946111-77-7

Printed in the United States of America

Dedication

I dedicate this book to anyone who has ever had something happen in your life that made you start all over again. Know that you may be delayed but destiny still is in front of you and you will get there. God's promises are true and absolute.

Your Plan B lies ahead. Let's go!

Acknowledgements

First, I acknowledge my Lord and Savior Jesus Christ for giving me all of my gifts and especially my gift to write His words.

My husband who is always supportive, loving and encouraging me to utilize all of my gifts and talents. Thank you honey.

To my mother, Dr. Daisy Foree, who is my number one cheerleader and always tells me, "hang in there, you can do it." To my father, Dr. Jack Foree, who is never far away from me in spirit or my heart. I only have to look in the mirror each day to see him.

To Rev. Claude and Mrs. Lillie Royston who support me in everything I do. Especially, Rev. Royston for his careful eye to detail and his sensitive heart to content.

To the rest of my family, I love you and thank you for your prayers, support and love.

Table of Contents

Dedication	iii
Acknowledgements	v
Introduction	ix
My Career Journey	1
The Yes	7
Happiness Looks Like	11
Wisdom With Age	15
Search Your Heart	19
Mind, Body & Spirit	23
What Changed?	27
Don't Burn Bridges	39
We All Need Money	45
Passion vs. Profession	49
Plan A? or Plan B?	53
What Can You Do?	61
All Gifts in Operation	65

Sacrifice. Hustle. Success.	71
Transition: Point A to Point B	77
Resources	83
Evolution is Ongoing	95
Reach Out for Help	99
About the Author	103

Introduction

I must confess that when I first started writing this book, I wanted to focus on speaking to teachers. Why? I was a teacher/librarian for 22 years until retirement in 2018. Given the rise of teacher strikes, sickouts, mass exit of people from the profession altogether, legislation that doesn't protect teachers as well as the seeming overall collapse in the support of public education, writing this book seemed only natural. By the way, I will support teachers and never forget how hard that job is no matter how many books I write, publish and promote. Teaching is the hardest and least appreciated profession I have ever been a part of, but I digress.

As I continued to write, I realized that teachers aren't the only ones who need to evaluate their lives, career choices, and future or potential entrepreneurial pursuits. Everyone does, no matter their job position or career choice. As a practice, I ask myself at least twice a year, if not quarterly, these three questions. Where am I? Where am I trying to go? What will it take to get there? Those three questions need to be given some long, hard and critical consideration in your life. Why? Because life is short.

I am not going to address each career sector, job choice or position in this short book. No matter if you are a teacher, janitor, engineer, computer specialist, lawyer, doctor, administrative assistant, film director, company CEO or anything in between, make sure that you are living the life that you were born to live.

Always have a plan. Amazingly enough, I am actually living my Plan A instead of Plan B. At 8 years old, I imagined myself traveling, singing, teaching and performing around the country. I saw myself with a band, singers and corporate sponsors, even though I couldn't even spell "corporate sponsors" at the time. I told my dad my Plan A, and he said, "No. College, career, marriage and then kids. In that order."

Fortunately, my heavenly father had another plan. He has helped me see that what I thought was Plan B was really what I wanted all along. I use the things in my Plan B everyday such as accounting, administrative skills, technology and my love of writing. My Plan B really is my Plan A. I have lived long enough to live out my dreams, passions and goals. It's a wonderful life. My job now is to encourage you to find out your Plan B…or was it really your Plan A all along?

Let's start and find out.

My Career Journey

"Teaching is the greatest career ever," my dad said. My sisters and I turned our heads and rolled our eyes. I can truly say my dad was a master teacher. When you are a teenager and you are in your dad's class for a workshop, and you walk out of the class feeling proud that you carry the teacher's last name, you know your dad is a fantastic teacher. I had to congratulate him myself. He loved teaching and it showed. My father said, "Be sure and get a minor in teaching because you never know." He eventually won and got two of us into the field of teaching.

But, in spite of my dad's love for teaching, he always did something else. My dad was bi-vocational in that he taught school during the day and ran a very successful janitor service at night. My mom took care of things in the day and had her own maid service in the daytime, and during the summer, we worked with her to make her job go faster and work day shorter.

I had planned to become an accountant, a CPA specifically. I have a bachelor's degree in accounting. My father didn't push us, and it took a minute, but my sister and I found ourselves in the teaching profession. I repeat, it took a minute.

I was a law/corporate librarian before I came to teaching. I was in divorced in 1994, finished my first master's degree in librarianship the same year, and found myself in my dream job at a Fortune 500 company. I worked there only two years before I heard God say, "Go home." Reluctantly, I obeyed. Crying and complaining all the way, I was home by the summer of 1996. I was ready to leave as soon as I got home, but I didn't realize I was headed back to school and that it would be right where I needed to be. I returned home to the only job I could get in librarianship, and that was at a private, all-girls high school, Presentation Academy. It was a strange place but a match made in heaven. It was my recovery, healing and launching place. I had to get a second degree because, you guessed it, I didn't have a degree, major or minor in education. I know, I know, don't scold me, and yes, my father was right, but this time I would get not only a second master's degree and doctorate, but also a degree in something more important. A degree in Purpose and Life.

I am an advocate and supporter of the teaching profession because I gave 22 years of my life to it. But, more importantly, I am an even bigger advocate for you living your best life with passion, precision and purpose. Do what you love and love what you do. It's not just a saying but a way of life. Why? Because as I get older, I realize that life is truly short. We don't have all the time in the world. People are cruel. Death's appointment is unknown, and we must live every day and every second like it is our last. That's my soapbox, and I proudly stand on it. But for this book, we've got to first ask ourselves some hard questions, get some real answers and make some hard decisions. Our lives depend on it and the lives of the people we love, lean on and lead are depending on it too. So, turn the pages and get out your tissues because you may cry or you may sweat, but we've got to get through this one way or the other. I'm here if you want to talk, so reach out to me at http://bit.ly/talkwithroyston.

In the meantime, let's get it done and live the life that we were born to live. Let's go!

What have you done the past 10 years in your current career?

_____

_____

_____

_____

_____

_____

_____

_____

_____

_____

_____

_____

_____

_____

The Yes

I said yes to teaching. Why? Teaching is a calling that came for me. I never pursued it; it came for me. Maybe I was marked for teaching by my father but I had to say yes to the job. I had to do the job well or they would have fired me. So maybe I was born for teaching but teaching really wasn't a desire for me. I didn't want to teach. For me, it was my assignment to teach. I enjoy teaching now more than ever because I am teaching what I love. I believe that is the reason why I could stay in teaching as long as I did because the subjects, literacy and technology, were great loves of mine. I was able to talk about and create a desire to love what I already loved. Now for the hard question for you.

Why did you go into your profession? What was the initial attraction? Why do you stay? Why can't you leave now or in the short-term future? We can't go forward into the horrible or bad parts of your job or career, the ills, the wrongs to eventually the things that are right with your career/profession/job until we address the why. So, think about it and answer the question within yourself first.

Why did you pick your profession? In the space provided, write out your why.

_____

_____

_____

_____

_____

_____

_____

_____

_____

_____

_____

_____

_____

_____

Seeing the words in black and white or in your own handwriting can be eye opening and an awakening of sorts. Re-read it and make sure that you didn't give the answer that you put in your portfolio or job application when you began your career. Furthermore, look at your answer again and make sure that it is not the "politically correct" why but the real why. Face the facts and be truthful within yourself. This is the time to walk in your truth and be the best you that you can be.

Happiness Looks Like...

Now you have your why, and hopefully, it was the honest truth. Let's go to the next hard questions. What do you want most out of life now? What do you think at this stage in your life would make you the happiest? I realize that you are asking yourself, "What does that have to do with making extra money to supplement my current career and/or professional income and give my family a better life?" Everything. Why? Because when you are able to find out what you really want out of life and pursue it, that will make you the happiest person on the planet.

I am not telling you or pressuring you to quit, abandon or walk away from your profession. Just answer the hard question of what would make you the happiest.

What does happiness look like to you in your life?

_____

_____

_____

_____

_____

_____

_____

_____

_____

_____

_____

_____

_____

_____

What do you want right now?

_____

_____

_____

_____

_____

_____

_____

_____

_____

_____

_____

_____

Wisdom With Age

At the time of writing this book, I am 55 years old. What makes me happy now is totally different from what made me happy when I walked into my first classroom in 1996 at 33 years old. I am not the same. I have faced things at 55 that I never thought I could face or conquer, but I survived. My drive, will and ambition are totally different at 55 than they were at 33. Why? I'm older, wiser and hopefully getting smarter each day. Also, I am focused on my goals and dreams now more than ever. Why? Because I can die and have been to funerals of people much younger than me, so I don't have time to waste, play or delay the gratification that I will attain in this thing called life.

So, I'm all in. I'm going for it. I'm going "hard in the paint," as they say in basketball, no matter what.

What makes you the least happy in your life right now?

_____

_____

_____

_____

_____

_____

_____

_____

_____

_____

_____

_____

_____

_____

What is one thing that you would change?

_____

_____

_____

_____

_____

_____

_____

_____

_____

_____

_____

_____

Search Your Heart

If I have no other impact with this book, I want one thing and that is for you to be honest with yourself. My purpose for this book is not to try to turn you into anybody that you don't want to be or aren't trying to be. I've already made that mistake by listening to others and not my heart. But as God would have it, I ended up right where I'm supposed to be. With that being said, I encourage you to search your own heart. Yes, be practical. Count up the cost of the project or undertaking. Ask questions. Do your homework. Email experts. Watch YouTube videos and jump in to Facebook Live broadcasts and get information.

Don't end up homeless on the street because you didn't do your homework or determine the risk. Yes, don't risk your health, family, career and life without a plan, but more than anything, go with your heart. I stayed in my job until retirement age and worked nights and every weekend by choice. It was the best thing for me, and I was committed to it and made the sacrifice for it. Again, this was my choice. You have some choices to make, and that's what this book is all about. Your choice. When you wake up every morning and look in the mirror, it's just you.

You are the most important person in your life. Right? What have you put in front of you?

_____
_____
_____
_____
_____
_____
_____
_____
_____
_____
_____
_____
_____
_____

What does your heart say?

_____
_____
_____
_____
_____
_____
_____
_____
_____
_____
_____
_____
_____
_____

Mind, Body & Spirit

When my father had a bible school on Monday nights, I took several classes from various professors, including one called "Incomprehensible God." One professor in particular talked about God being triune as the Father, Son and Holy Spirit, and that we were triune beings as Mind, Body and Spirit. My purpose for mentioning this is not for a theological debate or to determine your spiritual level, but to let you know that whatever decision you make regarding your life and future, all parts of you will need to be impacted. Your mind will need to be ready and functioning to complete the intellectual and thinking process of your operations. Your body will be at times energized, invigorated and alive. At other times, it will be a struggle to get out of bed because your body will be so exhausted from the amount of work that you will be putting in. Your spirit will be the wind, will power and strength to carry you through it all. Your ability to do all that is in your heart will not just come from your mind and body. Your spirit will be the driving force behind what you do.

Trust me, I know. So many times, I've literally had to pray for strength, and my spirit picked me up and encouraged me to move forward. I'm thankful for my family, friends, co-workers, mentors, coaches and preachers, but when it's all said and done, I have to put in the work myself, and so will you. It won't happen until you work it. Your mental, physical and spiritual health have to be in top shape for this journey. Additionally, there will be multiple times when you'll feel the need for renewal, revitalization, recovery and refreshing. Periodically and at times repeatedly on this journey you will have to stop, take a deep breath and recharge to keep going forward.

I'm not trying to discourage you to quit on the journey or even make you not start the journey, but I must be honest about what you are about to undertake. Everybody's journey will be different but anything worth having, doing or receiving will take effort, energy and endurance to complete. Let's go!

How is your health in Mind, Body and Spirit?

_____
_____
_____
_____
_____
_____
_____
_____
_____
_____
_____
_____

What Changed?

When I came to private and public education, I was the librarian. Books were always a love of mine, and I didn't have a hard time finding my way in the library world. But when technology was added to the mix in the library, I was in love. I found my real niche. I loved technology. In primary education, handling the book is still basic and must be for every child. I get that, but I was still thrilled and overjoyed with technology. I thought I would scream if I had to put another book away or reorder one because someone dropped it in a puddle or the "dog ate it." I didn't want to do that anymore, but I still loved my schedule. I still wanted to help teachers and not have my own classroom. So where did I go? The computer lab.

My last position in education was the school technology coordinator. I took care of all of the technology in the building, from the administrative offices to student computers. I was probably the most popular and the hardest-working person in the building, especially with the massive infusion of technology in today's classrooms. One day I was in my principal's office repairing his computer. I was sitting at his desk, and he said, "Mrs. Royston, you look good in that chair. Have you ever considered being an administrator?" I said, "No way. I've seen your job and I don't want it. I am most effective in the classroom trying to help kids." In my mind, I wanted to say that it appears that people forget about kids, teaching and the work it takes each day when they become administrators. I didn't want to forget.

So, before we think about entrepreneurship, what else can you do or become qualified for that would provide you more job satisfaction and/or more compensation? What does it take to do that job? What additional education, training or experience are required for that position? Who do you know that does that job already? Can you shadow them? Can you take them out for a Saturday morning cup of coffee or meet them after work to ask them about their position and whether it would fit you? You may not have to give up your career years and experience to start over.

You may just need to start over right where you are. The company may remain the same but the position within that company or career could change. Look around you. What else can you do? Where else can you thrive? What looks interesting that may require some research or obtaining some additional skills? Blossom right where you are. Evolve and reinvent yourself right where you are. It's possible but it's left up to you.

Reflection – Is the corporate or cultural system that you currently work flawed?

_____
_____
_____
_____
_____
_____
_____
_____
_____
_____
_____
_____
_____
_____

Can you change it from within?

Is there another position in your organization that you can apply for?

_____

_____

_____

_____

_____

_____

_____

_____

_____

_____

_____

_____

_____

Leave the company or corporation altogether or just move from within?

_____

_____

_____

_____

_____

_____

_____

_____

_____

_____

_____

_____

_____

Where am I?

_____
_____
_____
_____
_____
_____
_____
_____
_____
_____
_____
_____
_____
_____

Where am I trying to go?

What will it take to get there?

Who is there already that I can connect to?

_____
_____
_____
_____
_____
_____
_____
_____
_____
_____
_____
_____
_____
_____

Don't Burn Bridges

This was a saying of my father's, "Don't burn bridges." Why? Because you may need to cross that bridge again to ask for help, a reference or some general information. Be careful about venting your frustrations. Be sure the people hearing you can be trusted. While you are trying to figure out your life, find people who will be supportive and not go behind your back and make your professional life harder. One of the advantages of being the school technology coordinator or the itinerant teacher was that I touched base with every single person in the building, from the principal to the plant operator to the cafeteria staff to every teacher and every student.

The people that you currently work with know other people in the company/system as well as out of the company/system. So, consider your co-workers as a network, support system and team to help you fulfill your dream. Even if they don't know anyone directly, people are resourceful and probably know people who know people who can help get you where you want to be.

So, who is on your team? Who can help or would help or might help and you haven't even asked them yet?

Remember to reach out to people that are connected to a wide range of people. Don't forget the plant operator/janitor, the mail room people, cafeteria staff, security, drivers or other company-wide positions.

These people connect with people on all levels of the company/system. So, I ask again. Who is on your team? Who do you know that can help you with your dream?

Let's build your dream team, one person at a time.

Who is on your team now?

_____

_____

_____

_____

_____

_____

_____

_____

_____

_____

_____

_____

Who do you know that can help you with your dream?

_____

_____

_____

_____

_____

_____

_____

_____

_____

_____

_____

_____

_____

_____

What do you need to complete your team?

_____

_____

_____

_____

_____

_____

_____

_____

_____

_____

_____

_____

We All Need Money

I'm not trying to get all up in your business, but look at your finances and your lifestyle and your dream future. Do you just need extra money temporarily, or do you need a long-term increase in your income? Will a new position within your system or company help your situation at all, or will it just be a band-aid trying to keep back a rushing river? Are your children young, or are you an empty nester with no childcare needs and plenty of time and energy for additional tasks or a part-time job?

How much do you need to make your life better in the next month, 3 months, 6 months and beyond? Are your bills and income not meeting at all, or did an accident or incident make for a shortfall temporarily? You have to look at the situation honestly and determine your next steps. You may be able to do something in your current position for extra service pay and not have to take on something outside of the building. Either way, think about it and reflect on it in the space provided. Get out your bills, pay stubs and dreams and face the truth.

Let's go! Dream Life (Remember — Dream Big!)

What is Your Big Dream?

_____

_____

_____

_____

_____

_____

_____

_____

_____

_____

_____

_____

_____

_____

_____

_____

What are you doing toward achieving your Big Dream?

_____

_____

_____

_____

_____

_____

_____

_____

_____

_____

_____

_____

_____

_____

Passion vs. Profession

There is no judgment from me on the decisions that you make for your life. You have to do what you have to do. For me, I always wanted to be an artist and singer full-time. Instead, I chose to be safe, have a job and a career as a librarian/teacher. I don't have any children, but I like having money to pay bills and take care of other things in my life. I wasn't meant to live on the edge. The starving artist lifestyle didn't agree with me and how I was raised or wanted to live my life. That's my choice.

Once I gave myself over to my choice of being a teacher, it was easier to stay in the field until retirement than to get out and start over. I had to make that choice as well.

I had too many years in the system, and furthermore, the years to retirement were getting less and less. So, I decided to try other things on my own time and hold out until retirement. You may not have that same story and ability to wait or hold out, but I'm glad I was able to make that choice.

I did my passion of publishing, writing and singing in the evenings, every weekend and every break we got from school. I never gave up my passion; I just did it on the side rather than full-time. As a matter of fact, I was able to fund my passion with my profession.

At the end of the day, I'm proud of the choices I made for my life. It's time for you to make those same choices for your life. How will you fulfill your passion in life? Will you stay in a situation that doesn't fulfill you? Will you change your attitude, atmosphere or surroundings in your current profession and stay? Or will you plan to make a truly big move? The saying, "Do what you love and you'll never work another day in your life," is true. It's your decision. It's your life. Choose wisely.

What are you most passionate about?

_____
_____
_____
_____
_____
_____
_____

What are you doing now to fulfill that passion in your life?

_____

_____

_____

_____

_____

_____

_____

_____

_____

_____

_____

_____

_____

_____

Plan A? OR Plan B?

In my mind, Plan A is to stay where you are. That's fine. You have that option and can make that choice. Plan B is to try something new.

This is not a quick fix or an easy choice but you will eventually have to decide. Do you stay or plan to do something else or go somewhere else? It is up to you. As I stated earlier, there is no judgment here, but your life, happiness, family and future are at stake. I realize that there may be circumstances beyond your control that make it impossible or nearly impossible to do something different immediately, but think about it. With time, effort and planning, it can be done. It may not happen for you like it happened for someone else, but it can happen. Don't make any rash decisions that will leave you homeless or destitute, but make a plan, ask some questions, do your homework, save some money, get out of debt and then, slowly but surely, work that plan.

My Plan B was my Plan A all along. Honestly, I didn't have a plan but God had a plan all along and I just needed to say yes to His plan.

What will you say yes to? What will you decide?

_____

_____

_____

_____

_____

_____

_____

_____

_____

_____

_____

_____

_____

_____

What is the goal? Due Date for Completion.

_____

_____

_____

_____

_____

_____

_____

_____

_____

_____

_____

_____

_____

What do you need to achieve the goal? Hint: people, funding, certification, other resources, or changing locations?

_____

_____

_____

_____

_____

_____

_____

_____

_____

_____

_____

_____

_____

Who will hold you accountable?

What are your action steps?

_____

_____

_____

_____

_____

_____

_____

_____

_____

_____

_____

_____

_____

_____

What Can You Do?

My father always had a saying, "Always have something or do something that you can charge for." My dad always had a Plan B and sometimes C and D for projects, endeavors and life.

I didn't set out to be a publisher, speaker and author. I just wanted to sing. I enjoyed it, but my dad said, "Girl, you can't make money singing. You need a degree, career, job or something that is a sustainable and stable career." Then life, education, opportunities, connections to wonderful people, support of family and hard work allowed me to live a life of multiple gifts, talents, jobs and networks. My dad had my best interest at heart, but as I write this book, he has been deceased for nearly 10 years. So, time has changed everything. The stable jobs, careers or industries that we knew back then are fading away. "What can you do" is a major question that employers are asking potential employees now. Additionally, "What are you willing to do?" Furthermore, "What can you discover, create or invent to help us become a leader and transform our industry and world in the next generation and beyond?"

One thing I learned in the classroom is because curriculum is so structured, we don't have enough time or opportunity for discovery, imagination or to create something that doesn't exist. Science, research, development, testing, trials and errors are key to discovering new techniques and inventions. These things take time, and if we aren't allowed the time to discover, it won't happen.

So, I must challenge us to think not only outside the box, but outside the universe, for the next big thing, whatever that is. That next thing doesn't have a name yet, but it clearly will have a need that it's based on. Just ask what the needs are and you will find out more about the next.

So back to my original question, what can you do? The following is a very short list of things that can be the beginning of a business, career and new life, or as I've been calling it, your Plan B.

Teaching

Writing a book

Public speaking

Editing

Private tutoring

Founding a nonprofit organization

Consulting

Coaching/mentoring

Creating a new solution/product/service

Establishing your own business based on one of the above

Becoming certified in a different industry

Creating and patenting an idea

Inventing a slogan or saying and trademarking it

Design merchandising

Blogging

All Gifts in Operation

This is my new mantra for my life. All of my gifts, talents, skills, new skills, abilities, learned techniques and any other duties as assigned will be in operation during this season of my life. People who are gifted sometimes overlook their gift as just "something that I do." They don't realize that the gift that is naturally inside of them was designed to bless them and bless others too. For you, that natural gift, talent or ability could be your million-dollar moneymaker. I don't know everything that you can do, but in the words of my business coach, "Monetize everything." If people need what you can do, charge a fee and make money from that gift.

My natural gift is to sing. I sang for years in church and never received payment or asked for it. I just loved it. But then I changed my surroundings, mindset and circle of friends, and I now have several music CDs and people paying me to sing. I even established my own music publishing company, Juju 4ee Music, because I write my own music and am willing to license it for other people who do not write their own music. Monetize everything, I say, and let it bless me and other people. God blessed me to turn something that I was naturally gifted to do into a moneymaking activity. This is what it means to have All Gifts in Operation.

I confess that I don't want to go back to working a job. I don't want to have to punch a clock somewhere. I want to have all of my gifts in operation to generate income. I am willing to do whatever is legal, moral and enjoyable to make that happen. Why not you too?

So, let me help you. A gift is something that you don't have to work for or put forth much effort to do. A gift is something that you do naturally and do it well. Sure, your gift should be developed and polished, and your presentation on point and correct, but it's a gift. What's your gift? If you don't know, ask someone. Be sure that it is someone who loves you unconditionally but will be honest with you and tell you the absolute truth. Ask them, "What am I good at?"

What are your gifts?

_____
_____
_____
_____
_____
_____
_____
_____
_____
_____
_____
_____
_____
_____
_____
_____
_____

What gifts can you monetize?

How much will people pay? (Note: do your homework. Research the market.)

_____

_____

_____

_____

_____

_____

_____

_____

_____

_____

_____

_____

_____

_____

Sacrifice. Hustle. Success.

The word sacrifice is a curse word to some people. There are some people unwilling to make any sacrifices, period. In my life, I am willing to make the sacrifices necessary to be successful. I will not be one of those people who looks back on life and has regrets or wonders what would have happened if they had just done whatever they had always wanted to do but never did. I'm not going to be one of those people. I am have decided to go for it no matter what. I make adjustments for things that don't work. I take naps, go on dates with my husband and take short trips for fun, but I'm also on my grind every single day in one way, shape or form. Even if I am in discovery mode, I am working on something.

Now I know there are people who make huge sacrifices for their family, friends and job. I have and will probably make more of these sacrifices for the people in my life in the future, but more importantly, I want to make some sacrifices of wasting time, hanging out and doing nothing for me.

I don't watch a lot of television. I have cut my shopping down to only what is necessary. I travel but there is always a business motive. I go to bed early and get up early to make the most of my day.

My sacrifices plus my work ethic plus my wonderful clients plus GOD and my husband equals success. Plain and simple. I don't believe that you get anything for free. There is a cost even if it is sweat equity/pricing/tax. Nothing great comes from no effort or work. I just don't believe it. There is no magic formula. The magic is in the doing, striving, working, sacrificing, learning, growing, failing, falling, getting back up, trying something new, moving away from some people, meeting new people, trying something old that worked and then trying something else new.

Success looks different for me and it will be different for you too. That's okay. I don't have to be like you and you don't have to be like me, but what I do want for you is for you to be the best, happiest and most successful you that you can be. Don't settle. Don't give a job all of you and look for a thank you and a plaque, but walk away with a purpose, plan and profit of your own. It's possible. I'm living proof that it can happen.

I love my life. I enjoy the freedom of setting my own clock, pitching my own products and services, traveling to meet new clients and meeting new people that turn into new clients. That is exciting to me. I'm living my best life. It's not the easiest life, but it is mine and I am grateful to God every day when I wake up.

I am striving each day not to compare myself to anyone else. Sure, I keep up with people that are in my field, but overall, I'm me and I like me. The sacrifice plus the work equals success to me. What about you? You have to answer these and other questions for yourself. My job is to propose the question; only you have the answers for your life.

What are you willing to sacrifice for the life that you want?

_____

_____

_____

_____

_____

_____

_____

_____

_____

_____

_____

_____

_____

_____

_____

What does success look like to you?

_____

_____

_____

_____

_____

_____

_____

_____

_____

_____

_____

_____

_____

_____

Transition: Point A to Point B

For 12 years, I went to work at a school that was 45 minutes from my house. I drove in the rain, ice, snow, sleet, hail, potential tornadoes and everything that the weather could throw at me. Indiana and Kentucky built a brand new bridge over I-65, one of the busiest highways in the United States, which caused hours of delays and leaving early to avoid being late to school most days. There were accidents, near misses from other cars and countless debris in the road ways. Add detours, onlookers of other accidents, oversleeping, flat tires, colds, flu and other emergencies that prevented me from getting to work. I know that you get the picture, but I want you to know that in your transition into your new endeavor, whatever that is, look for similar things to happen in your life as well. There will be weather, detours, distractions and people that will get in your way. There will be onlookers that won't stop to help but just slow down to look, shake their heads at the struggle and just drive away.

I want you to know that when the struggle is real, when you are weary, when you have no help and limited resources, that is all normal. Go back to the beginning of the book and re-read the parts about your passion, your why and personal mission in life. Sometimes there will be loved ones and friends who will encourage you and offer help, but at the end of the day, the vision, mission, project, business or invention was given to you. You are in transition. The journey is long and not a short sprint. You have to keep your eyes on the prize, goal and mission. I'm not saying that no one will come help you; that is not always true. But, if NO ONE comes, you've still got to go. Transition is painful. Transition is scary. You are unsure in transition. Going from being an employee with most things taken care of, questions answered, handbooks written, systems in place and money secured to being an entrepreneur is scary, filled with uncertainty and many moments of doubt and sleepless nights. But keep going.

Transition is unstable mainly because you can't leave where you are and you're definitely not where you want to be yet. Stuck in the middle is where I found myself most of the 12 years working a job and building my business. I never really was "all in." I had to wear a lot of hats and hope that I didn't put on the wrong hat on the wrong day and use it at the wrong time. In my business, I decide how the money is spent, what direction to go and what products or services to create. When you work for someone else, they decide. They determine what will happen and what will not happen in this building or at this company. If you don't like it, you can leave.

If you don't like something in your business, you can change it, quickly. If you don't change, you could lose everything. Leaders, bosses and CEOs make swift, sure and calculated decisions. To be successful, you will have to make that transition from employee to CEO. If you want to be a boss, you have to act like one until you can fully become one.

Surround yourself with the best information, people and resources in transition. Don't go it alone. Reach out. Make connections. Ask questions so that you can make the best decisions. Transition is hard enough in the best of circumstances, so don't transition without as much knowledge is possible. The key to transition is training. In the words of my elders, get all you can and can all you get.

Are you in Transition?

_____

_____

_____

What do you need in the transition? Ask. Seek. Find.

Resources

Let me start this section by saying that you do not have to sign up for and start paying for all of these services or even one of them immediately. Look at the list. Read through the list, do your research and then determine what you need and CAN afford right now. Yes I am yelling with the capital CAN because I don't like it when coaches and mentors yell at people about what they must do in their business and when, but then they are not there to help pay the bills, go to the grocery store, clean the house, take care of the kids and love the husband. Everything has to be in stages. I do suggest that you consider — yes, consider — these services, and when you are ready and can afford it, pray, do your homework and pay for the ones you need.

Website — The first thing I had for my business was a website. I built a simple website for just my music before I wrote my first book. I have always had my own real estate on the Internet. Before social media, before an email marketing system, I had my own website. I built it myself with basic software and maintained it myself. I still maintain my own sites to this day. Why? I'm a tech geek. Additionally, people could search for me on the Internet, find out information about me and contact me without me having to answer my phone, which I couldn't do while teaching in the classroom. Make it easy for people to find you.

Business Cards/Post Cards — I've always had business cards. I first printed my own business cards on a dot matrix printer. I can still hear that sound of the ribbon and sizzle sound going back and forth to print on that paper. I spent hours creating business cards. The main reason was so I could have a way for people to contact me easily.

Email and Phone — I still have my first email address from 15 years ago, jforee@gmail.com. I still use it to this day. Why? Because people have been contacting me for more than 15 years and I don't want to change it. Those people may still need to contact me for something. I have also had the same phone number for more than 20 years as well. If at all possible, don't change your phone number. Use a Google Voice number that is free with a Gmail account and will keep your personal phone private. If you are concerned about privacy, start out in business with the Google Voice number.

Social Media Scheduling — Because I taught school, I couldn't be on social media all day, but I did want to post to my social media. Thus, I purchased a scheduling service. I could schedule my posts for the next week on Saturday or Sunday and it posted my information, flyers, upcoming events, encouraging posts and anything else I wanted to post while I worked. I use Hootsuite but there are so many more out there. Do a Google search, put together a list, and pick the best one for you.

Email Marketing — There are multiple email marketing systems out there to choose from. I recommend that you choose one that can integrate with your website. Try not to pick a website service that doesn't integrate with another service. Why? Because you will be doing double the work, and that's not the point of any of these services. The point is to make sure that it makes your job as easy as possible, especially until you can transition to entrepreneurship full-time. Read the fine print. Check the help and support pages before you sign up and create anything.

Text Marketing — According to the Pew Research Center, as of the writing of this book, 95% of Americans have a cell phone of some kind. 77% of Americans have a smartphone which can do a multiplicity of things including many apps for business. So, what better way to market to people than through their cell phone number? If they provide you with their number, utilize it. Most people will see the ad on their phone before email. There are a multitude of companies that provide text marketing services. It may not be at the top of your list of services to purchase but should be on the list of future options for marketing and promotion.

E-commerce Store — Because I travel so much, I usually sell a lot of merchandise as I go from place to place. But now I realize that I can't physically be everywhere at the same time. I need to be able to make money and send people to a place to purchase materials while I am asleep and while I am on the move. I love to travel but there are times that I have to stop, recover and rest. On the other hand, there are still bills. Some website templates come with a store feature already attached. If possible and within your budget, do it. Maximize the potential of your resources, products and services through an e-commerce store. Let's go!

Virtual Assistant — Following up with clients. Routine administrative tasks. Assistance at events. Social media, website and email maintenance. Eventually you are going to need help, even if it is getting help while you are still working another job or on the weekends. Do your research. Be sure that they understand what your needs are, and that you are getting your needs met, for a fee that you can afford. Don't bite off more than you can chew. If you can't afford it, get your family and children to help you. But don't leave a virtual assistant off the list of things that you will eventually need as you grow your business. That type of support is essential.

Build a Team — For me, building a team has been a slow process. Some people build a team faster than others. I admit that I have control issues and have been slow to bring people outside of my family into my business affairs. As I have grown, I realize that with confidentiality agreements, non-disclosure agreements and other contracts, it is possible to bring others on board to help with many tasks. Do your homework, get referrals, make your expectations clear including payment, duties, tasks and other duties as assigned and get the help that you need.

Video (Pre-recorded or Live) – I have pre-recorded videos and posted them via my social media scheduler and received the feedback later. This is a good way to build connections with your target audiences and markets.

Video (YouTube Channel) – I cannot tell you how much business and how many contracts I have received from YouTube, especially in my singing career. I have my husband record me singing, and we upload the videos to my YouTube channel so people can actually hear me and see me singing. I want people to know what I look like when I am coming to their church or event for the first time. I was contacted by a church regarding singing during eight performances during the Christmas season. I asked them specifically, "Do you know what I look like?" They said, "Of course. We want to hire you. We just to know if you are available for these dates and at this level of payment." My answer, "Yes." Boom. Thank you, YouTube!

    These are not all of the tools, services, skills, apps or resources that you will need in your business or life. There are people right now inventing more convenient ways and methods to enhance your life. Keep on the lookout for new things every day, follow the trends and the successful people in your industry or field, research the trends, and know what your budget is and stick within your budget. In the end, you will be able to determine what you need, why you need it and succeed by it.

Which resource do you want to begin working on?

_____

_____

_____

_____

_____

_____

_____

_____

_____

_____

_____

_____

_____

Evolution is Ongoing

Entrepreneurship, especially if you are trying it for the first time, will be a trying time in your life. There will be constant learning, growing, revising and moving in your new direction. Don't get too down on yourself if you don't get it right the first time. That is so normal, and I know that I have probably already said this a hundred times, but you are on a journey and not on a supersonic jet scheduled to arrive at a specific date and time. It doesn't happen that way. I'm sorry. I wish I had some magical formula, but I don't. I will tell you that nothing will happen if you do nothing. I take that back, something will happen, and that something is nothing. Something else will happen and you will be more miserable, unhappy and unfulfilled if you are not actively moving in the direction of your dreams and destiny.

So, throughout the process, there will be ups and downs and curves and rocks. It will amaze you how much you will get done and the people you will meet on this journey. Keep going and keep learning.

Finally, remember Elton John's song "Circle of Life" from the movie *The Lion King*. Life is a circle, a cycle, and it goes around and around. Business is the same way: cyclical and circular. There will be good days and bad days, but if you keep moving, evolving, learning and growing, the good days will outweigh and be more frequent than the bad days. You are on an evolutionary journey. You will be constantly changing and evolving into the person that you want to be. Don't quit. Don't give up. Don't stop. Keep evolving, and ultimately, evolve into the best life ever.

Evolve. What does that mean to you?

_____
_____
_____
_____
_____
_____
_____
_____
_____
_____
_____
_____
_____
_____
_____

Reach Out for Help

In the teaching profession, there are annual professional development sessions, workshops and conferences that must be attended to retain your license as a teacher. There are other professions that have the same requirement. Entrepreneurship doesn't have that requirement, but I urge, plead and strongly encourage you to have a coach and mentor. Also, invest in at least one course/workshop/retreat/conference that will help you with the implementation of your next steps.

I'm here for you.

Questions. Information. Courses. Coaching. Mentoring. Books. Consultation. Reach out.

This has been one of the key things that I've tried to emphasize in my business and in this book. Get help. Don't go it alone. My contact information and places that you can connect with me are listed below.

Let's go!

Julia Royston

P. O. Box 4321

Jeffersonville, IN 47131

502-802-5385

bkroystonpublishing@gmail.com

www.bkroystonpublishing.com

www.juliaroyston.net

Schedule an appointment http://bit.ly/talkwithroyston https://my.timetrade.com/book/X7YC2

Store – http://bit.ly/bkroystonstore or https://writers-and-creative-arts-academy.thinkific.com/

Facebook - @juliaroyston

Twitter - @juliaakroyston

Instagram - @jujuroyston

LinkedIn - @juliaroyston

What do you need help with first?

_____

_____

_____

_____

_____

_____

_____

_____

_____

_____

_____

_____

About the Author

I spend my days doing what I love, which is writing, publishing, speaking, coaching and singing. Helping people tell their story, introducing these stories and demonstrating how to best monetize their message and purpose is my "Why." Every gift, ability and avenue that is within my reach are the conduits that I use to spread the love of reading, writing and inspiration messages around the world. In my spare time, I love to travel, be a cheerleader for other champions and live my best life along with my husband. Follow me on social media or visit www.juliaroyston.net or www.bkroystonpublishing.com.

www.ingramcontent.com/pod-product-compliance
Lightning Source LLC
Chambersburg PA
CBHW031635160426
43196CB00006B/426